Fly Away Peter

When Peter the budgie says he wants to leave his safe, comfortable cage and fly out into the big wide world, his friend Julius the sparrow thinks he must be crazy, but promises to help. Peter finds the world a very strange place, full of all sorts of dangers he'd never imagined. He soon learns that not everyone likes budgerigars (though they all call him a pretty boy!), and that for some, he's just a tasty meal. He has to sleep where he can and eat what he finds. But he makes a lot of new friends and Julius and Benjy are with him. But Peter's not just a pretty boy. He can talk like a human and this saves him from many a bad situation. He learns that one way to stay out of trouble is to make his enemies laugh.

Then one day, he looks through a window and sees a green budgie singing happily in a cage. That's when he decides enough is enough and home is best after all.

By the same author:

When the Wind Blows
Birds of a Feather
Flight of Fancy

Fly Away Peter

Linda Allen

Illustrated by Gerald Rose

A Grasshopper Book
Abelard · London

First published 1979 by Abelard-Schuman Limited

ISBN 0 200 72604 8 (Hardback)
ISBN 0 200 72605 6 (Paperback)

Abelard-Schuman Limited
A Member of the Blackie Group
Furnival House, 14–18 High Holborn
London WC1V 6BX

Printed in Great Britain by
Thomson Litho Ltd, East Kilbride, Scotland

Contents

1

The Great Decision

"Who's a pretty boy, then?"

Peter made no response.

"Come on, Peter—who's a pretty boy, then?"

Peter watched as his owner turned and left the room. "If they say that to me just one more time," he declared to his reflection in the mirror, "I shall fly away."

"You wouldn't dare," said a voice from outside the window. "You're a budgerigar. Budgerigars can't live in the big, wide world."

Peter fluttered about excitedly. "Is that you, Julius?" he called.

A brown house sparrow appeared on the window sill. "Yes," he said, "I thought I'd just come along and see how you were getting on, and a good thing I did, talking like that. You ought to be more careful about what you say, Peter. You never know who might be listening."

"Does it matter?" enquired Peter in exasperation. "I can't stand it in here much longer, with those great faces staring in at me and their 'Who's a pretty boy, then?' I've got to get away from here, and I don't care who knows it."

"That's all very well," retorted Julius, "and I can quite see your point of view, of course, but you must be more careful, especially if you are serious about flying away. Suppose a sparrow-hawk had been listening out here, instead of me—what do you think would have happened?"

"I don't know."

"Well," said Julius, "any sparrow-hawk that I've ever met would have jumped at the chance of taking a tasty budgerigar just to make a change in its diet, so it would have waited outside until you did escape, and then—pounce!—just like that! You'd hardly have tasted freedom before the sparrow-hawk had tasted you."

"I didn't think of that!" exclaimed Peter.

Julius peered into the room, and just for a moment he wondered why any bird with such a cosy place to live in should ever think of flying away from it. Then he saw how little space there was for Peter to move around in, and he understood why the budgerigar was longing to escape.

"It's very good of you to come visiting me like this," Peter was saying. "Why do you do it?"

"I like your company."

"It's very kind of you to say so, Julius, but would you still like my company if I got out of here? Birds of a feather, you know, and all that?"

"Well of course I should!" cried Julius. "I should be proud to be seen with you."

"And would you teach me all the dangers of the big, wide world? Tell me what to do out there? What dangers to look out for? Would you really help me, Julius? You see, if I do come out I shall

need a friend like you."

"I'll help you in any way I can," promised Julius, "but I'm warning you that it isn't easy living out here. I wouldn't want you to think that. No nice cosy cages, you know. No seeds put out regularly for us. No protection from cats and hawks and all the other dangers there are out here."

"I'm willing to risk all that," Peter told him, "just for the sheer joy of being able to spread my wings and fly away to freedom. The people in here are well-meaning, I've no doubt, and they are kind to me in their way, but my nerves are all on edge, and they don't really understand. I must go, Julius, I really must."

"Well, I can see that you're quite determined," sighed Julius, "and I can sympathise with you, but there's one thing that really worries me about all this."

"What's that?"

"Well, it's your colour."

"My colour?"

"Yes. You're blue."

"I know I'm blue. How could I ever forget it? Do you know, the one in the brown waistcoat, who cleans out my cage—Max, I think, is his name—wanted to call me Bluey. I ask you! Bluey! I was very glad when the one with yellow hair said she didn't like it and that as far as she was concerned my name was Peter." He shook his head. "Why should my colour worry you, Julius?"

"Because it makes you so conspicuous. There

are plenty of blue birds out here in the wild, but none quite as bright as you are. A colour like yours could lead to all sorts of complications. But," he went on hurriedly, seeing Peter's downcast expression, "I'm still willing to stick by you."

"Oh, thank you, Julius. I want you to know how much I appreciate that. If only you knew how I enjoyed talking to another bird you might understand what it's like in here, listening to all those silly phrases they keep bombarding me with day and night. After all, what's it to me that Mary had a little lamb? I don't even know Mary. And you've no idea what a fool I feel when they keep coming and saying 'Who's a pretty boy, then?' "

"Yes, I suppose it must be very embarrassing," agreed Julius, unable to repress a chuckle in his throat. "What else do they say to you?"

"Oh, lots of things," replied Peter. "The latest one is 'God save the Queen'. Oh, how she does go on at me with that one! And then there's 'Max is coming!'—that's not too bad, being a perfectly straightforward observation. But the worst one of all . . ." He broke off in embarrassment and turned his head away.

"Yes? Tell me," urged Julius, with a twinkle in his eye.

"Well, if I tell you," responded Peter with a quick glance at his friend, "it will only be to illustrate how stupid they must think I am."

"Surely not!" cried Julius, not quite losing the twinkle.

Peter edged nearer to the bars of his cage. His voice dropped to a whisper, so that it was only barely audible through the gap at the top of the window. "I tort I taw a puddy tat," he said.

Only for an instant did Julius glance backwards and down into the garden, then he laughed out loud. "They don't really try to teach you baby-talk, do they?" he cried.

"Yes they do!" said Peter indignantly. "I wouldn't mind so much if they merely said 'I thought I saw a pussy cat', but the other is nothing more or less than an insult."

"Oh dear!" said Julius, doing his best not to laugh again. "Whatever do you say when they try to teach you that sort of rubbish?"

"I say it right back in their faces," said Peter, "just to show them how silly it sounds, but all I get for my pains is to hear them say what a clever little birdie I am."

"I should very much like to stay and hear some of that," said Julius.

Peter looked towards the door of the room. "Now's your chance," he said. "The one with yellow hair is coming now. Just keep perfectly still in the corner. When you hear what she says you'll understand why I want to get away for a while."

Julius waited. A shadow crossed the room and a human voice said, "Hullo, Peter—who's a pretty boy, then? God save the Queen. Give us a kiss!"

"Poor Peter!" exclaimed Julius to himself. He waited, expecting Peter to respond with one of the same phrases, but to his surprise Peter said something quite different.

"Seven-eight-three-o-six-five-one."

The human voice reacted in a startling manner. "Oh, what a clever little birdie!" it said. "Reminding me that I must make a call! *Such* a clever birdie!" And the shadow re-crossed the room and disappeared.

"What was all that about?" asked Julius.

"Oh, just a little trick I've discovered," said Peter modestly. "If I say that to her she sometimes goes away and talks to herself out there instead."

"How extraordinary!" exclaimed Julius, listening. Sure enough, the human voice came to them from the other side of the door, talking to itself. "Quite apart from all that," went on Julius, looking sympathetically at his friend, "I suppose you must get awfully lonely for bird company at times?"

"Oh, I do! But, you know, Julius, when I do feel like that and I call out to the birds outside to come and talk to me the people in here think I'm *singing!*"

"Never!"

"They do. They quite go into raptures over it. Why can't they understand? The more I *sing*, as they call it, the more lonely I am."

"Well, I shall make quite sure that you have plenty of company in future," promised Julius stoutly. "I shall tell every bird I meet to come and call on you occasionally."

"That won't be necessary," said Peter, suddenly sticking out his chest and stretching his toes.

"Why not?"

"Because I have quite made up my mind," was the reply. "I shall fly away tonight."

"Tonight?"

"Just before the sun goes down. This is exactly the sort of day when they let me out for a few minutes of an evening. Quite often they leave the window slightly open, just as it is now, because they think I haven't got the sense to squeeze through the gap, but tonight I shall. Will you wait for me, Julius?"

"Of course I will."

"I'll fly over to the old dead tree at the bottom of the garden. Meet me there."

"All right," agreed Julius, beginning to feel almost as excited as Peter himself, "but do be careful. Remember the sparrow-hawk."

"I'll remember," said Peter.

2

The Big Wide World

"It's very big," said Peter.

"What is?" asked Julius.

"The world. I can hardly see the end of it."

Julius stared at him. "But that isn't all there *is!*" he cried. "The world is a million times as big as this! If you went on flying for the rest of your life you wouldn't see it all. There are rivers and mountains, and seas, and lands beyond the seas. Didn't you know?"

"No," said Peter, "I didn't know all that."

"You're quite sure you want to stay outside?" asked Julius anxiously. "You don't want to go back inside?"

"No." Peter looked at the green fields spread out below the tree in which they had come to rest. "I couldn't go back now. There's so much I want to see. Just give me a little more time to get used to it, that's all. I'll be all right." Nevertheless, he shivered a little.

"Are you feeling the cold?"

Peter admitted that he was. It was summertime but he wasn't used to having so much fresh air all at once. Besides, the sun was going down.

"Fluff out your feathers," suggested Julius.

"Like this?" asked Peter.

"That's right. Does that feel better?"

"Yes, it does. How clever you are, Julius."

"I'm not clever. That's something that all wild birds know."

Peter edged a little closer to his friend. He was beginning to realise how much he needed him.

"We must find a place to sleep tonight. The sun's almost gone, now, and we're a long way from my usual roost. A building of some sort would be best for you, I think. They're warmer than trees."

They were just about to fly away in search of one when they heard a sound behind them. Turning, they saw another house sparrow.

He was looking very much the worse for wear. Two or three of his tail feathers were missing and several others were sticking out at all the wrong angles. "Benjy," said Julius sternly to the newcomer, "you've been fighting again."

Benjy looked rather guilty, but he said defensively, "It's not my fault, Julius, that other birds *will* come and sit on my tree."

"It isn't your tree, Benjy," retorted Julius. "I've told you that before. Nobody can absolutely own a tree. It isn't *done*. A bush, yes, nobody disputes ownership of a bush with a nest in it, but not a whole tree. You're far too ambitious for your own good sometimes." He turned to Peter and explained, "This is my young brother Benjy. He's always fighting."

"Not always," said Benjy cheekily. "I'm not

fighting now."

"You know what I mean," said Julius. "You ought to stop this aggressive behaviour of yours. You know Mother doesn't like it."

"She won't know unless you tell her," responded Benjy, "and if you tell her I shall jolly soon let her know that you've got a blue friend."

"It doesn't matter what colour my friends are," said Julius, "and it's very rude of you to say such things in Peter's presence."

"That's all right," said Peter patiently, "I understand."

"I'm blessed if I do," said Julius. "Sometimes I can't believe that he came from the same parents, even if he was a second brood."

When Peter had spoken so gently Benjy had begun to look at him with more interest. "I'm sorry," he apologised suddenly. "I wouldn't behave so badly if only Julius would let me come with him. I *like* to be with Julius, but he gets cross when I follow him around."

"If you acted in a more responsible manner . . ." began Julius, when Peter interrupted.

"If you don't mind, Julius," he said, "I should really be glad of Benjy's company as well as your own. I should feel more—more secure."

Julius nodded his understanding, and Benjy, with complete lack of restraint, said, "I know what you are, Peter. You're a budgie."

"That's right," said Peter.

"Have you escaped from somewhere?"

"Yes," said Peter, "just a short while ago."

Benjy gave a short whistle. "No wonder you look so anxious," he said. "It must feel ever so strange for you out here."

"It does, rather," agreed Peter. "We were just going to look for a place to sleep."

Benjy, looking for the moment more experienced than his older brother, said, "I know just the place. The old barn."

Julius stared at him. "What old barn?" he asked.

"On the other side of the river," said Benjy.

"Do you mean to say that you have been over the river all by yourself?" demanded Julius.

"It's just like flying over any other place," said Benjy.

Julius gave a sigh of exasperation. "You know what Mother said," he cried. "She said that there was a big white ghost-bird over there and that any bird that happened to see it would be turned to stone."

Benjy was unimpressed. "I didn't see any ghost-bird," he said, "and I don't believe that birds can be turned to stone. Mother picks up the most stupid stories from those gossiping friends of hers, and I wish she wouldn't listen to them."

Julius retorted that his brother ought to have more respect for his mother, but Peter was looking anxiously at the darkening sky. "Do you think we ought to go?" he asked suddenly.

"Where?" asked Julius.

"To the old barn."

Benjy looked pleased. "You really want to go there, Peter?" he asked. "You'd like me to take you?"

"Yes," said Peter, looking at Julius for encouragement.

"Very well," said Julius. "You fly on the other side of Peter, Benjy, and I'll fly this side."

"Thank you," said Peter. They all took off and flew steadily towards the river, which, as they drew nearer, had an eerie look about it. A light mist drifted slowly above the water, strange birds cried from the rushes along its banks. "Is it very far?" asked Peter.

"Just over there," Benjy reassured him, for he could see that Peter was tired. The farthest he had ever flown before was round the room where his cage had been kept.

The old barn was a completely derelict building standing in open farmland. Peter was glad that he had friends with him, for he wouldn't have cared to fly into such a place on his own. The twilight cast eerie shadows on the walls, and strange noises came from the old beams as unseen creatures stirred behind them. Peter had the feeling that hundreds of eyes were staring at them, but whether those eyes belonged to mice, or rats, or other birds, he had no way of knowing. He followed Benjy on to a narrow ledge and settled down for the night.

Darkness fell rapidly. After a while Benjy said in rather a small voice, "I've never been here in the dark before."

"And I don't suppose you'll ever want to come in the dark again," hissed his brother. "Couldn't you have suggested somewhere a little less creepy than this place?"

Peter said nothing at all. He had never in his life been anywhere like this. He had been used to central heating and soft lights, to a cover over his cage at night, through which he knew no enemies would creep. It was very different here. He thought about the ghost-bird that Benjy had mentioned, and he began to tremble.

What if there really was such a bird? In the atmosphere of the old barn anything was possible. The noises up above were getting louder, more insistent. There were hissing sounds, shufflings, scratching . . . "Can't we get a little nearer the place where we came in?" he pleaded suddenly, but before his companions had time to reply something terrible happened.

Out of the corner of the barn there suddenly appeared a great white shape. It came quite silently, gliding on wings that seemed to require no propulsion. It had enormous, staring, dark eyes. It had a strangely human face.

"The ghost-bird!" whispered Julius. "Don't look at it—don't!"

"It's too late!" cried Benjy. "I already have!"

Peter was so afraid that he could hardly move a muscle. "I think I'm turning to stone," he moaned.

"Follow me!" cried Julius bravely. He took off and flew towards a place that was open to the stars. Benjy followed him. Peter, however, was so confused and so frightened that he flew the wrong way and, when he tried to turn, the ghost-bird was blocking his way, so he flew in quite a different direction. It was only after several anxious seconds that he found a way out. He flew as far from the barn as he could, not suspecting even for a moment that he might be flying in the opposite direction from that taken by his two friends. When he glanced backwards to see if they were following him his blood seemed to turn to ice. He gave a little shriek of terror.

The ghost-bird was following him!

3

The Ghost-bird

It was no use; he could go no further. He sank down on a branch of a tree and shut his eyes tight so that he might not look upon the terrible shape of the ghost-bird that was even now coming to rest beside him. He called in vain for his friends to come and rescue him. He even called out to his human friends in the hope that they would hear, but they were far away, and his cry of "Mary had a little lamb!" quavered into nothingness on the still night air.

"No, she didn't," said an indignant voice beside him. "She had a big fat toad, and even that didn't satisfy her."

Peter thought about this for a while, then he opened one eye and took a quick look at the ghost-bird. He shut his eye again and wondered if all ghost-birds were as substantial as this one appeared to be.

"Before that," went on the voice, rather wearily, "she had a vole, and a mouse, and a little bit of something tasty I picked up in the farmyard. I can't think where she puts it all."

Peter opened both eyes. The ghost-bird was gazing into space. "I'm a budgerigar," said Peter, almost apologetically, "so perhaps you find it rather difficult to turn me to stone?"

"I wondered what you were," said the ghost-bird. "That's why I followed you. I don't think I've ever seen a budgerigar before." He paused for a moment, and then went on, "Do you particularly *want* to be turned to stone?"

"No," said Peter.

"That's just as well," was the response, "because I haven't the foggiest notion how to do such a thing. What makes you think I can?"

"Just something I heard," said Peter quickly, thinking it best not to pursue the subject.

"What's all this about Mary having a little lamb?" asked the ghost-bird. "If she has, then somebody else is feeding her besides me. I never gave her lamb." He stared at Peter with his dark eyes. "Mind you," he said suddenly, "it wouldn't surprise me."

"What wouldn't?"

"If somebody else was feeding her. She's got the most enormous appetite."

"Who has?" Peter was becoming very bewildered.

"Mary."

"Oh!" Peter gasped. "Do you know Mary?"

"Of course I do. She's my wife. She's incubating the eggs, so I've got to feed her. I tell you, I'll be jolly glad when the eggs are hatched and she can go out and fend for herself again."

Peter breathed a sigh of relief. "I don't believe you're a ghost-bird at all," he said.

"Ghost-bird? Me? Who said that?"

"Oh someone I heard of. It doesn't matter now. They said that any bird that looked at you would be turned to stone."

The bird made strange noises, opened his beak as wide as it would go, and disgorged a pellet. "Prod me," he said.

"What?"

"Prod me. You'll soon find that I'm no ghost."

Peter gave him a cautious prod.

"Well?" said the bird.

"I knew you weren't a ghost," said Peter, not altogether truthfully. "My friends thought you were, but I didn't believe it—not really."

"Nevertheless," said the bird, "there *are* stone birds, not very far from here, as it happens. That might be how the story got around. Would you like to see them?"

Peter hesitated. "I think I ought to find my friends first," he said.

"We'll give them a call," suggested the bird, and he gave such a sudden, loud shriek that Peter jumped several inches into the air.

"I don't think they'll respond to that," he said. "You've probably frightened them away for good. What kind of a bird are you, anyhow?"

"I'm a barn owl. My name is Barnaby. What's yours?"

"Peter."

"All right, Peter, you'd better call for your friends in your own way, but if they think that I am a ghost-bird it isn't likely that they will hear you, for they will be miles away by now."

"You're probably right," agreed Peter sadly, but all the same he thought there was no harm in trying, so he cried out all the human phrases he could think of, knowing that the two sparrows would recognise them if they heard them as being spoken by a budgerigar. There was no reply to his calls, however, and as they perched there side by side listening for a response, another voice broke in.

"I'll tell you what," it suggested. "If you'll go away and your friends come looking for you I'll tell them where you've gone. Disturbing everybody at this time of night. It's a disgrace. Nobody's had a wink of sleep since you two arrived."

"Who's that?" demanded Barnaby sharply.

"Never you mind who it is," replied the voice. "Here I am in my hole, minding my own business and trying to get some rest, and what happens? Birds shouting at the tops of their voices, waking everybody up and frightening the poor little fledglings half to death. Why can't you go to roost like decent, law-abiding birds?"

Barnaby sighed. "I'll never be able to understand this night-sleeping," he said, and in a louder voice, "We're going to see the stone birds, if anybody asks."

"You should have gone there in the first place," returned the weary voice. "With only a little more effort you might have managed to wake *them* up, too."

"Woodpeckers," nodded Barnaby with conviction. "Only woodpeckers can be as sarcastic as that. Come on."

He spread his beautiful wings and took off without a sound.

"No wonder people think you're a ghost," said Peter, hurrying to catch up with him. "You don't make the least little bit of noise when you're flying, do you?"

"No. It helps with the hunting, you see."

"Hunting?"

"For food."

"Oh yes, food." Peter was beginning to feel hungry himself. "Shall I have to hunt for food, too, Barnaby? I've only just got out of my house, you see."

"Hunt for food?" repeated Barnaby, glancing back at Peter. "I shouldn't think so. You look more of a seed-eater to me. Isn't that what they gave you?"

"Yes," said Peter, "but I don't know where to go to find seeds."

"I'm sorry I can't help you there," said Barnaby. "The only thing you can do is wait until morning and look out for some of the finches. Plenty of them about—they'll help you."

Peter thanked him for his advice and they flew on. They were now approaching a long, grey building set in a curve of the river amid wild flowers and tall grass. The building was roofless, and there was no glass in any of the windows, but in the moonlight it looked beautiful. "What is this place?" asked Peter curiously.

"I've heard it called The Priory," replied Barnaby, "but I couldn't tell you what that means. It's very old now, of course, and, I may add, a very good place for beetles."

"Beetles?" echoed Peter.

"Mary is very fond of beetles," Barnaby told him. "I think you should inform your friends that she much prefers them to lamb."

Peter was just thinking that he wouldn't be informing his human friends of anything ever again, when he saw the stone birds. They were really only the heads of birds jutting out from the wall of The Priory—hawk-like heads with cruel beaks and protruding eyes. He thought of what Julius had told him about the sparrow-hawks, and he shivered. "If you didn't turn them to stone," he asked, "who did?"

"Nobody did," replied Barnaby, but without any trace of scorn for Peter's ignorance. "They were carved by humans out of stone, long ago, so long ago that nobody remembers who did it."

Peter took another look. "How clever!" he exclaimed. "They look so real, especially with the moonlight shining on them." His eyes twinkled and, with an air of bravado, he hopped on top of one of the heads and looked down the long, curved beak. "I'm glad they're not real," he added.

"So am I," said Barnaby. "I can't stand the hawk family myself."

After inspecting all the stone birds Peter began to feel very weary. "I shall have to rest, Barnaby," he sighed. "I'm not used to flying long distances and the darkness makes me drowsy."

Barnaby was beginning to look restless. "I can understand that," he said in a kindly voice, although his eyes were searching the ground and crevices in the walls (probably for beetles, thought Peter). "If I were you I should stay here for the night. You wouldn't be afraid would you?"

Peter looked round. "No," he said bravely. "I quite like this place."

"Then I'll show you a corner where you'll be perfectly safe. Come over here." And Barnaby showed him a place where swallows had started to build but for their own reasons had abandoned the site. "That should suit you."

Peter crept in. "Yes," he said gratefully, "this is just right."

"I've got to go now," said Barnaby, "but if I meet the blackbird just before dawn, as I generally do, I'll ask him to put the word round that you're here. It's sure to get back to your friends before the day's very old."

"Thank you," said Peter.

When Barnaby had gone Peter settled himself comfortably in his niche and fell fast asleep.

4

Attack!

Peter was awakened in the morning by a great commotion. He opened his eyes and saw that he was being attacked by a group of four or five dark blue birds with pointed wings and forked tails. "Get out of our nest!" they were shrieking. "We built it, we built it! Go away!" They flew rapidly round in circles, occasionally swooping down on the nest and fluttering their wings so close to Peter's face that he could scarcely breathe. They seemed to be taking it in turns to execute this dive-bombing action, and their concerted efforts terrified the poor budgerigar, who had never experienced anything like it in his life before.

"I'm sorry," he gasped. "I didn't know you wanted it. I'll leave at once if you'll only move out of the way."

"Who said you could sleep in our nest?" demanded one of the swallows as he swerved round.

"The—ghost-bird," stammered Peter without thinking.

"Ghost-bird?" cried another of the swallows. "There's no such thing. Don't try to be clever with us."

"I mean Barnaby," said Peter, becoming more

afraid every minute, and he tried to push himself back against the wall in order to be out of the way of those rapidly-flashing wings. Oh, what he would have given at that moment to be back in his cage! He was hungry and thirsty and friendless out here in the big wide world.

"Who cares about Barnaby?" screamed one of the birds. "You're the one we're concerned about. Who do you think you are, taking over another bird's nest? Didn't they teach you any manners where you came from?"

Peter was in such a confused state of mind that the bird's final question led him to say quite suddenly the first phrase that came into his head. "Max is coming!" Perhaps it wasn't manners, but it was something they *had* tried to teach him where he came from—surely that would do?

Instantly the birds ceased their screaming. One or two of them gave a final swoop down, as if in a final warning, and then, to Peter's amazement, they disappeared round the angle of the wall.

"Excellent!" said a new voice. "What a clever bird!"

"Clever boy, clever boy," said Peter.

"Are you lost?" went on the voice. Turning his head a little Peter saw a starling with a friendly face looking down at him from a perch above his head.

"Not exactly," replied Peter.

"Well, I must say it was rather clever of you to get rid of them like that," went on the starling, and she hopped down on to a lower ledge in order to get a better look at Peter.

"Get rid of them like what?" asked the bewildered Peter.

"By saying that Max was coming."

"Don't they like Max?" asked Peter, rather wishing that Max would come along and take him home, for by this time he was quite faint with hunger.

"Of course not," was the amazing response. "There's nothing that Max likes better than a tender young swallow for breakfast."

"I don't believe it!" cried Peter, suddenly feeling loyal towards his owner.

"Believe what you like," shrugged the starling, "but don't blame me if the sparrow-hawk suddenly fancies *you* for breakfast."

"Oh I see!" said Peter casting a quick look upwards. "Max is a sparrow-hawk!"

"Of course."

"I thought you were talking about another Max," said Peter, with a sigh of relief.

"Do you mean that there are *two* sparrow-hawks?" cried the starling. "If so, I must go and warn my friend the robin."

Peter decided that it would take too long to explain about Max, so he changed the subject. "I'm very hungry," he said. "Do you think you could put me in touch with the finches? I was told that they might be able to help me to find some food."

"Certainly," said the good-natured starling. "Come with me."

Peter hesitated. He explained a little about himself. "So you see," he concluded, "I must wait here in case my friends come for me. The ghost—I mean Barnaby—was going to see the blackbird about me first thing this morning."

"No problem," responded the starling cheerfully. She gave a curious whistle. Two more starlings appeared. "Wait here for Peter's friends the house sparrows," she told them, "and tell them to wait here. He'll be back when he's had some food."

The greenfinches to whom the starling introduced him were kindness itself. They showed Peter where the best feeding places were and gave him all sorts of useful tips on how to open seed pods and husks, which kinds of seeds were the tastiest, and which ones to avoid. Peter ate his fill, and after thanking the greenfinches for their hospitality he flew back to The Priory.

To his delight he found Julius and Benjy waiting for him there, having encountered the blackbird as they searched for Peter on the other side of the old barn.

They were amazed to see him looking so confident and cheerful, for they had feared the worst when the blackbird had said that he had last been seen at The Priory perching close to a huge stone bird. Peter told them all that had happened to him since he last saw them.

"Not a ghost-bird?" said Julius in a hushed voice. "A real bird?"

"A barn owl," said Peter.

"I never saw a barn owl before," said Julius. "I'm sorry, Peter. A fine friend I turned out to be."

"That's all right," said Peter. "I didn't expect you to know everything about everything."

"I told you," broke in Benjy suddenly, "I told you there was no such thing as a ghost-bird, didn't I?"

"You were pretty scared last night when you saw it," retorted his brother.

"We were all scared," laughed Peter. "Let's forget about it. I want to see some more of the big, wide world." Now that he wasn't so hungry and the sun was shining, his spirit of adventure was returning. They were just deciding where to go next when Benjy nudged his brother. "Look who's coming," he said.

"Who is it?" asked Peter.

"Bessy the blackbird," said Julius.

"Full of her own importance," said Benjy.

"Can't bear to miss anything," added Julius.

"Nosey," nodded Benjy.

Bessy came down on the ancient wall beside Peter, and without waiting for anybody to speak, burst out, "Who's this?"

"Our friend Peter," replied Julius.

"What are you doing out in the open?" she demanded.

"I escaped," said Peter.

"That was very rash, wasn't it?" she said. "I suppose you're having all kinds of trouble out here?"

"Not really," said Peter. "I'm managing quite well, in fact."

"Are you indeed? Well, just you wait till the winter comes, young man. You'll begin to wish, then, that you were back in your nice cosy house. Do you know what snow is?"

"I've seen it," said Peter. "It looks quite pretty."

"I daresay it does," cried Bessy, nodding her head vigorously. "I daresay it does, from inside, when you're nice and dry, and warm, and you've got food and water. But what about when you're out here, eh? When the grass is all covered over and there's nothing to eat. That's the time to be thankful for human friendship, I can tell you. Why, last winter I don't know what I would have done without Mrs Plenty, who put food and water out for me every day."

"Who's Mrs Plenty?" demanded Benjy, thinking that he might bear her in mind next winter.

"You must know Mrs Plenty!" cried Bessy. "She lives in the big red house where the fields begin—on the other side of the river—you must know it, because I've seen you over in that area many times, if I'm not mistaken. You're the one who's always fighting."

"What did I tell you?" frowned Julius.

Benjy grinned. "I've turned over a new leaf."

"House sparrows have no business to go turning over leaves," snapped Bessy. "Anything hiding under a leaf belongs to me."

"I don't understand," said Peter.

"I don't suppose you do," retorted Bessy. "There must be lots of things that budgerigars don't understand. You can't be expected to understand, either, coming from the other side of the world."

"The other side of the world!" exclaimed Peter. "I really don't think I did."

"It's a well-known fact," snapped Bessy, "that budgerigars come from Australia."

"I'm sure I would have remembered if I had," said Peter hesitantly, not wishing to offend a lady, but remembering, from somewhere in the back of his mind, that he had come not from Australia, but from a place near Nottingham. "But it doesn't matter where I came from," he added, "because my friends are looking after me very well."

"I'm very glad to hear it," said Bessy, giving him a thoughtful look. "Where exactly is your house?" she asked.

"On the other side of the river," Peter told her.

"Beyond the trees?" asked Bessy sharply.

"Yes," said Peter.

"Anywhere near the big dead tree?"

"Exactly there!" cried Peter, excited without knowing why.

"That's part of our territory!" cried Bessy. "We always feed in Mrs Plenty's garden." She hesitated for a moment, her eyes fixed steadily on Peter's. "Do they leave much rubbish out?" she enquired.

Peter was surprised. "Rubbish?" he repeated.

"Yes. You know. Rubbish left out for the men to collect in their big green monster."

"I really don't know," replied Peter, looking in confusion at his two friends.

"What had you in mind?" asked Julius, equally mystified.

"A nice bit of polythene," replied Bessy, her eyes gleaming.

"*Polythene!*" said all three little birds together.

"What on earth is polythene?" added Julius.

Bessy gave a deep sigh. "Well, I can't expect a house sparrow to know," she said. "You take so little trouble over your nests, compared with us blackbirds, but I can assure you that there is nothing, absolutely nothing, like a bit of polythene woven into a nest to keep out the rain and cold. It's a sort of paper."

"Oh, I see!" said Benjy. "You were wondering if we had noticed any of this stuff lying about over there! You're building a nest!"

"That's right."

Julius broke in. "Well you may be lucky," he informed her, "because last night, when I was waiting for Peter in the big dead tree, I saw someone come out of the house and take a box full of papers down to the place where they sometimes light a fire."

"I'll go there at once!" said Bessy, spreading her wings. "I'm very much obliged to you, I'm sure." She hurried off, her voice coming back to them as she flew, "Take my advice and go back home, Peter. You don't belong out here."

"I wish blackbirds wouldn't do that," said Julius disapprovingly.

"Do what?" asked Benjy.

"Scream out like that when they're flying away from you," said Julius. "It's so vulgar and ill-mannered. She may be right about our nesting habits, but we could certainly teach her a thing or two about behaviour."

Peter looked round at the golden world. "Well, never mind about Bessy now," he said. "Let's go and explore. There's so much I want to see!"

5

The Birch Wood

"Isn't it exciting?" said Peter. "What a marvellous place to play hide and seek in!" The three birds had come to a birch wood, attracted by the cries of many different species. Peter hopped about from one branch to another, peeping under the leaves and peering into holes in the trunks of the trees. "No wonder there are so many birds in here," he went on. "I never imagined a place as interesting as this. What's wrong?" he said suddenly, noticing that the other two birds were staring fixedly towards the centre of the wood.

"There's something going on in there," said Julius. "Shall we go and find out what it is?"

"Yes!" responded Peter at once. "I'd like to go and make friends with all the other birds."

"It depends what kind of birds they are," said Julius cautiously. "Just stay quiet for a moment, will you, Benjy?" he said to his brother, who had been chirping away to himself for the past three or four minutes. "I want to find out who's there before I go barging in."

Benjy listened. "That's a chaffinch," he said, "and a robin."

"There's a crow there as well," said Julius doubtfully.

"And a magpie."

"But lots of house sparrows, too," said Julius, making up his mind, "so we might as well go and find out what all the noise is about."

Peter and Benjy followed him, and were surprised to find quite a gathering of birds in one tree, all nodding their heads and talking at once. When the birds saw the three friends, however, they fell silent for a moment and regarded them with suspicion. "This is a private meeting of the wood-dwellers," they said. "What do you want?"

"Nothing," stammered Benjy. "We wondered what was going on, that's all."

"None of your business," snapped a large black and white bird with a red crown, glaring angrily at Peter, who began to wish that he hadn't come.

"We're not doing any harm," protested Julius. "We're just looking, that's all."

"Why?" snapped a beautiful jay.

Before any of the three strangers could speak a small flock of light brown birds began to flutter round Peter, taking an occasional peck at his feathers and saying that he had no business to be there without an invitation, and who did he think he was, anyway, flaunting himself like that?

"He's a spy," hissed a large black creature with huge feathery legs. "Get rid of him."

"Never trust a bird with a beak like that," cried another.

"We're all short of breeding space as it is," said one of a group of bluetits. "What with hedges being chopped down every day, and old walls dismantled that we've nested in for generations, we can't afford to have foreigners coming in here and taking away our space."

"I'm not a foreigner," protested Peter. "I'm a budgerigar."

"A what?"

"A budgerigar."

"That proves you've got no business here," said someone in the back of the crowd. "The situation is desperate. We can't have new birds coming in here. That's what this meeting is all about. The old orchard fell yesterday and the place is full of big yellow monsters today. Those old trees were full of insects—valuable food for birds like us, especially in the breeding season. Last week it was the old field behind the mill that went—next week who knows? There was a time when strangers were welcome here, but that is no longer the case. We simply can't afford hospitality now."

Suddenly Peter was very frightened. The big black bird was closing in menacingly and there was a hostile look in his sharp eyes, but neither Julius nor Benjy had made a move, so Peter stood his ground with them and looked appealingly at those birds that seemed less hostile towards him. But no-one spoke up in his defence.

"If that sparrow over there says one word more about pretty little birds in blue rompers," hissed Benjy, "I shall go for him."

"No, Benjy, no!" said his brother.

"Don't make trouble," pleaded Peter. "Let's just go quietly away."

"They won't let us," whispered Julius. "We shall have to be very careful or those flycatchers will mob us."

"What shall we do?" said Peter, beginning to tremble all over.

"Fight 'em!" said Benjy, still glaring at the house sparrow.

Unfortunately the sparrow heard him. "Fight whom?" he asked haughtily.

"Anybody who says we've no right to be here," retorted Benjy, "or anybody who makes insulting remarks about my friend Peter."

"So you're Peter," said the sparrow, looking at the poor little budgerigar, who was thinking about his cage again. "I thought you were the queen of the may."

"God save the queen," said Peter apologetically.

"He talked like a human!" cried some of the birds, crowding in upon him and demanding to know where he had learned to speak like that.

"Dresses like one, too," said the sparrow scornfully.

"Don't you dare speak to my friend like that!" cried Benjy, taking a peck at the other bird's neck.

"We're only defending what is ours," said the other, pecking back.

"He doesn't want your territory," retorted Benjy. "He's a cage bird. He's spent all his life locked up in a house. How would you like it?

And then to come out at last and receive this kind of treatment. You ought to be ashamed of yourselves, all of you."

Some of the birds began to look sympathetic, but the sparrow had gone too far to back out of his argument without losing face, so he closed with Benjy, and the two birds fell to the ground, fighting furiously.

"We didn't know you had been a prisoner," spoke up a chaffinch, looking quite ashamed. "You should have told us straight away."

"You didn't give us a chance," said Julius.

"We thought you were spies," said a wood warbler.

"I still think that one is a spy," said the huge black bird, walking menacingly along the branch where Peter was perching.

"Nonsense," snapped Julius, "he's nothing of the kind."

"Of course he isn't," cried Benjy, who had won the battle and was flying up to join the others. "Anybody can see that."

"Well done, Benjy," muttered Julius.

"You're not cross with me for fighting?" asked Benjy in surprise.

"Not on this occasion," said Julius. "I was very proud of the way you defended Peter."

Benjy stuck out his chest and intimated to all the other birds that he would take on any three of them that dared to attack his friend Peter again. But the rook was edging closer to Peter, who was

watching his approach with terror. He really thought that the rook was going to bite him, or sit on him, or something equally dreadful.

"Well?" said the rook, glaring down at him. "What have you to say for yourself, eh?"

Once again, Peter became lost in confusion. He started to explain in bird language who he was, but somehow it was all his human phrases that kept popping up in his mind. Which one would please this extraordinary bird? Which one would bring the approving "Clever boy, clever boy!" from this bird's mouth? "God save the Queen," he said again, but that didn't do the trick. The rook took a final step towards him. He had half-spread his great wings; his shoulders were hunched; his head thrust forward, almost touching Peter's own.

Peter trembled. He looked up into the bird's face and in a voice that seemed loud in the silence, said, "Give us a kiss!"

Instantly, there was complete pandemonium. Peter was amazed. Birds fell about all over the place, laughing and clutching at each other with merriment. They held their sides. One song thrush, who for years had been trying to take that same rook down a peg or two, fell on her back and kicked her legs in the air. "Oh!" she spluttered, gazing up at the rook, who was stalking about trying to regain some of his dignity, "Oh, I'm so glad I came to the meeting! I felt sure that it would be all the same boring old stuff, but I never thought anything like this would happen!"

Peter was staring at the other birds wondering if they had gone mad. It was quite a surprise to him that so many of them understood human language, for he didn't realise that many of them were habitual listeners to human conversations; that they sat on the roofs of houses and heard everything that was going on indoors; that they perched innocently upon the branches of trees and often heard things they ought not to hear. He couldn't help feeling rather sorry for the rook's embarrassment, and in order to ease the bird's feelings he said soothingly, "Pretty boy, then, pretty boy!"

This only made matters worse. The birds screeched louder than ever, and the rook departed in a huff. It was several minutes before order was restored, when the thrush, still giggling, flew up and perched beside the bewildered Peter. "You have no idea," she said, "how glad I am that you came."

"Really?" said Peter.

"Oh yes, these meetings are apt to be very tedious, you know. Somebody's always calling a meeting about something or other, but as we can never agree on anything they're always a waste of time. Where did you learn to say things in such a droll way?"

"My humans used to say them to me all the time," said Peter.

"Oh do tell us some more," begged the thrush.

"Yes, please do," chorused the bluetits, now thoroughly ashamed of themselves for being so jealous of Peter.

"All right," agreed Peter. "I don't know if it will amuse you, but there is one thing I used to hear, and as it seems to be about time for an afternoon nap, how about, 'Time for beddy-byes!'"

Once more the birds went off into peals of laughter. "Come along," said the song thrush after a while. "Time to call off the meeting. Time for beddy-byes!" And all the birds departed, leaving Peter and his two friends quite alone in the silence of the birch wood.

"I didn't think it was as funny as all that," Peter said reflectively. "After all, the one with the yellow hair used to say it to me every night when she put the cover on my cage." And for a moment there was a touch of sadness in his eyes as he realised that he would never again hear it said to him. The cage, after all, hadn't been such a bad place.

"Well?" said Benjy. "Shall we stay here? Or would you like to go and look at the river?"

Julius glanced at Peter. "If it's all the same to you, Peter," he said, "I think we should go to the river. Benjy looks as if he could do with a bath after all that scuffling on the ground."

The three birds took off and flew through the dappled wood in the direction of the river.

6

A Bird with Green Legs

The sun was beginning to decline when Peter realised how hungry he was. Seeing something rather tempting hanging from a tall stem he began to peck at it, and discovered to his delight that it was rather good. Benjy and Julius amused themselves by nibbling at whatever came in their way, for sparrows are not very particular about what they eat. The day wore on.

They had come to a place where the ground was marshy, with reeds and other water plants growing in profusion. For some time the birds had been aware of strange sounds coming from the depths of the reeds; now they decided to go and investigate them. As they drew nearer to the sounds, however, Julius drew back a little. "I'm not sure about that 'kik-kik-kik-kik' noise," he said. "You know how I dislike strange noises."

"Then why don't you fly up and investigate?" asked Peter. "Whatever it is, it seems to be staying on the ground."

"I'll go," said Benjy, beginning to spread his wings.

"No!" cried Julius. "This is the sort of place where a trap might be laid."

"What kind of trap?" asked Peter in alarm.

"There are many different kinds of traps," Julius informed him, "but the worst one of all is a man with a gun."

"With a gun?" said Benjy, closing his wings with a snap.

"What's a gun?" asked Peter.

Julius told him. Peter was horrified. "Why do they want to shoot down birds?" he enquired in a whisper.

"I have no idea," was the reply. "I only know that they do it, so you see it's best to proceed with caution. If we fly up into the air we might wish we hadn't."

They crouched quite still for a few minutes, each thinking his own thoughts, until Peter said, "Is it always like this in the big wide world?"

"Like what?"

"Being happy and carefree one minute and scared to death the next."

"Oh yes."

"It's the scary part I don't like," said Peter.

"Ssh!"

The kik-kik-kik was almost upon them. Peter stared in fascination at the direction from which the sounds were proceeding. Somehow he felt that the noise was not unfriendly, and when he glanced at Benjy he saw that he, too, was looking interested rather than concerned.

"I don't think it's a bad noise," he ventured to remark.

"Maybe not," said Julius cautiously.

"It's a voice," said Benjy.

"I never heard a voice like that," said Julius.

"I did," said Peter. "It came out of the talking box in the living room, but it never got out, so I never found out what it was."

Suddenly the reeds parted. The first thing that the birds saw was a pair of red eyes, followed by a long red bill. At least, thought Peter, it's a bird. A great, long-legged bird, it was true, but a bird all the same. He wasn't going to be afraid of it. He had survived the encounter with the barn owl, and then the rook, and was still in one piece, so he would stay where he was and make conversation.

The bird had caught sight of them now, and he stopped short in surprise. Sparrows he had seen before, but not a budgerigar. He stared at Peter with friendly eyes, and encouraged by his look, Peter said, "Hullo, we're not trespassing, are we?"

"Oh no," said the bird, "I don't mind little birds like you. Where have you come from?"

"Over the river," replied Peter.

Julius, who had been trying to remember what kind of a bird this was, suddenly remembered quite well. "Are you a moorhen, by any chance?" he enquired.

The moorhen cackled. "Well, I am a moorhen," he replied, "but I don't think it was by chance. I suppose the reason was that my mother and father were moorhens, too, so you see I didn't have much choice in the matter. Now you," he went on, "are a house sparrow—I know that much, but your friend seems to be of a new species." He looked enquiringly at the three birds, waiting for more information about Peter.

"I'm a budgerigar," said Peter.

The moorhen looked pleased. "Are you now?" he said. "I've heard about budgerigars and I've always wanted to meet one..."

"You've got green legs!" said Benjy suddenly. He was staring at the moorhen in fascination.

"Benjy!" remonstrated his brother.

The moorhen cackled. "That's right," he said. "Two of them."

"Peter escaped from his house yesterday," Julius said, and went on to introduce himself and his brother.

But Benjy was still enchanted by the moorhen's legs. "I wish I had green legs," he said wistfully.

"For my part," interrupted Julius with a frown in his brother's direction, "I have always wanted to see a moorhen."

"And now you have," chuckled the moorhen, who really was a most affable chap, "and I have seen a budgerigar."

"It must be *wonderful* to have green legs," sighed Benjy.

"Benjy!" cried Julius again. "Don't you know that it's very rude to talk about people's legs?"

"I don't mean to be rude," protested Benjy. "I really do think green legs are beautiful and I'm only telling the moorhen how much I admire them."

"I accept your esteem," bowed the moorhen with a twinkle in his eye. He turned to Peter. "Are you going anywhere in particular?" he asked conversationally.

"No, not really," replied Peter. "I'm just enjoying my freedom, thank you. At least, I'm enjoying it most of the time. I have had a few unpleasant moments, but I'm told that a bird must always be prepared for those." He glanced round. "Is it safe here? I mean, is it safe for us to fly up?"

"Oh yes," the moorhen assured him, "this is a private stretch of water and the man who owns it is very fond of wild life, so you needn't be afraid."

"I think this would be a very pleasant place to live," said Peter.

"It is," said the moorhen, "but only for waterfowl. I should think you three would be better off in the meadows. I'm told that it's very pleasant over there." And he inclined his head in the direction he was thinking of.

Julius thanked him for his advice and said he hoped that they hadn't disturbed him.

"Oh no," the moorhen assured him, "I was only patrolling my territory as I usually do when we have eggs."

"Eggs?" said Peter.

"Then we'll leave you in peace," said Julius. "Come along, Benjy."

The two sparrows were on the point of taking off when they noticed Peter. He was staring straight ahead of him as if he had gone off into a trance, and the two brothers were quite afraid that there was something wrong with him. "What is it, Peter?" asked Julius anxiously. "Don't you feel well?"

"I don't know," answered Peter, as if he were in a daze, "I have a most peculiar sensation."

"Where?" asked Benjy and Julius together.

"All over."

"But what can have caused it?" asked Julius, and then he caught in his breath. "That stuff you were eating back there. Are you sure it was all right? You haven't been poisoned, have you?"

"No, I don't think it's that."

"Then what?" asked the moorhen, hoping that it wasn't anything he had said.

Peter blinked and drew in a trembling breath. "I know it's going to sound silly," he said, "and I do hope that you won't laugh at me for saying it, but, the truth of the matter is that I have never seen an egg!"

"Never seen an egg!" The other birds looked at Peter with great sympathy. A bird— and he had never seen an egg! The moorhen lost no time. He turned, and said over his shoulder, "Follow me."

After a few moments they all stopped. "There you are," said the moorhen, "there are my eggs. You must excuse my wife—she's very shy, and I expect she ran away when she heard you coming."

Peter gazed down at the eggs in their shallow nest of reed grass. "Oh!" he breathed. "Oh, how beautiful!"

"They are rather special, aren't they?" said the moorhen with pride.

"I should just think so!" sighed Peter. His heart was beating fast. "I've always tried to imagine what eggs were like, but I never thought that they would look like this." And he gazed at the eggs as if he would never take his eyes off them again.

"You've got nine!" said Benjy, who had been counting. "I never saw nine eggs before, not all in one clutch. And to think that when they hatch they'll all have green legs!"

The birds laughed. Then the moorhen cocked his head on one side and said, "Excuse me, but my dear wife is getting anxious, so if you wouldn't mind . . ."

"Of course not," responded Julius. "We must go. It was nice meeting you. Goodbye."

"Good luck with the eggs," said Peter.

"And good luck to you, Peter. Have a nice day."

"Thank you."

"By the way," the moorhen called to them as they left, "you'd better find a good roosting place tonight. There's rain coming. I can always tell. Try the old boathouse . . ."

"Rain?" said Peter to Julius as they flew over the river. "I don't like the sound of that. I don't think I shall like being out in the rain at all." He glanced up at the sky. "Do you really think it will rain tonight?"

"There isn't a cloud in the sky," said Benjy carelessly.

"All the same," said Julius, "I think we should start looking for a place to shelter. The water birds always seem to know when the rain is coming."

"There's a place over there!" cried Benjy suddenly. "Do you think that could be the old boathouse?"

"Let's go and investigate," said Julius.

7

The Teller of Tales

"Before we go in there," said Julius cautiously to the other two birds as they sat surveying the boathouse from the branches of an old elm tree, "I think we ought to make quite sure that it's a safe place."

Peter looked more carefully at the boathouse. It was a large, wooden building. Its roof was still intact and the place looked quite sound, except that the double doors had fallen off their hinges and were lying half in and half out of the shallow water. It was evident that the boathouse had not been used for a great many years, for tall reeds had encroached upon it and were growing right inside the building. A half-submerged boat was just visible, too, in its innermost depths, and as Peter watched, a mallard duck came paddling out of the shadows, followed by a brood of ducklings. They sliced their way through the water weeds and disappeared round the far side of the boathouse. A more peaceful scene it was impossible to imagine. "I'm sure it's all right," said Peter.

Julius nodded. "It would certainly be a good place to spend the night," he said, "especially if there's rain on the way."

"The moorhen wouldn't have recommended it

if it hadn't been safe," said Benjy.

Still Julius hesitated. He had Peter's safety to think of, as well as his own and Benjy's, for hadn't he promised to take care of him? He was just about to suggest that the other two waited whilst he flew over to investigate when he stiffened. "Listen!" he hissed.

Benjy cocked his head. "Warning cries!"

The cry which had reached the ears of the two sparrows suddenly multiplied, grew louder, became a shrieking chorus: "Max! Max! Max!"

"Max?" murmured Peter, thinking of his human friend.

"The sparrow-hawk!" cried Julius, searching the sky with his sharp brown eyes.

"I can't see him anywhere!" said Benjy.

Peter, too, looked up. The sky seemed empty, except for a few clouds which had gathered on the eastern horizon. Max was being cunning; he was flying low so as to surprise the three crouching birds, and he suddenly appeared, skimming over the alders which were growing beside the water. "Into the boathouse!" cried Julius urgently. "Follow me!"

Peter had learned his lesson in the old barn and he didn't intend to make the same mistake again. He fixed his eyes firmly on Julius's tail and followed it. They were only just in time. Max's shadow fell for an instant between them and the sun, and then they were in the boathouse, looking for a place to perch. They finally settled on one of a number

of beams which supported the roof. "That was close," said Benjy.

"I wonder which one of us he was after?" mused Julius.

Peter said nothing. He was thinking that the big wide world was sometimes a very unpleasant place and that if he had had anything to do with it there wouldn't have been any sparrow-hawks in it at all. He crouched there in the semi-darkness until he had recovered his composure and then he looked round. He and his two friends were not the only occupants of the boathouse; there were at least a dozen starlings perching on the beams, all curiously facing in one direction, like human beings waiting for a concert to begin. "Perhaps they are," said Peter out loud.

"What?" said Julius.

"Perhaps all these birds are waiting for something to happen," whispered Peter.

"They certainly look as if they are," agreed Julius.

"I'll ask," said Benjy, and he nodded affably to the nearest starling, whom he had heard addressed as Pickles. "Is this a private gathering?" he asked, remembering the incident in the birch wood.

"Not particularly," replied Pickles. "We starlings like to get together in the evenings, but we don't mind anybody joining us. You're quite welcome."

"Thank you," said Benjy gratefully, and Peter heaved a sigh of relief and settled himself more comfortably on the beam. "Are you waiting for anything in particular?" went on Benjy.

"Yes, we're waiting for The Teller of Tales," was the surprising reply.

"The Teller of Tales? Who's that?" put in Julius.

"He's a starling who comes from beyond the white hill. We don't know much about him except that he has spent his whole life flying from one place to another in a search for stories to tell, and that when he has a new one for us he sends word that he is coming."

"And he's coming tonight?" asked Benjy.

"The messenger said so."

"Perhaps he would be interested in Peter's story," suggested Julius.

"I'm sure he would," said Pickles. "That was the first thing that entered my head when I saw you fly in."

There was a stir among those birds nearest the entrance and a murmur went through the little crowd. "Here he comes!"

At first sight there was nothing unusual about the newcomer. His plumage, though well-cared-for, was not out of the ordinary; his bill was no brighter than that of any of the others; but there was a look of great experience about him. He had travelled far. He had had many adventures. His eyes seemed to reflect some of the strangeness of the places he had seen.

The Teller of Tales had rested at the entrance

to the boathouse and the last rays of the setting sun had fallen directly upon him. He knew the effect of a dramatic entrance. For a moment or two he stayed quite still, looking backwards along his own flight-path, then he made his way to the centre of the crowd and bade them all good evening. He had a special look for Peter, who knew that he had been marked out as a certain source of interest, but he said nothing to him then.

The first few spots of rain began to fall on the roof of the boathouse, like a roll of drums announcing the commencement of the entertainment, and The Teller of Tales began.

"There will be those among you," he said dramatically, "who will not believe what I am about to tell you, but I give you my word that there is a written record in human language which bears out my story."

Nobody spoke or moved; he had already captured the attention of every one of the birds in the boathouse; not least of all Peter, who was staring at him in breathless anticipation.

"Some days ago," went on The Teller of Tales, "I found myself listening to a conversation between two sheep." He hesitated and looked round at his audience. "Now if anyone disputes that I could actually understand a conversation between sheep, or, indeed, that sheep *can* converse, let them leave at once. Very well," he continued when nobody made a move, "I will tell you what those sheep were saying."

Peter suddenly remembered something about sheep, but he thought it best not to bring it up at that moment, so he waited for The Teller of Tales to continue.

"It seems that many, many years ago one of these sheep had an ancestor in the county of Devon into whose fleece a bird had woven its nest! A living fleece, mind you, not the fleece of a dead sheep!"

There was a gasp from the crowd. The Teller of Tales looked at Benjy and said, "What do you think of that, young sparrow?"

"I think, sir," retorted Benjy with a grin, "that it must have been a very sensible bird, for only think how warm and cosy that nest must have been."

"No doubt it was, young sparrow, no doubt it was, because, you see, not only did the bird build there, but it also hatched and fledged its young in there."

"What kind of a bird was it?" enquired Pickles.

"It was said to be a linnet, but there was no absolute proof of that. However, it was recorded in a newspaper of the time, and also in a diary which, said the sheep, is still kept in a museum for anyone to see. The story itself had been handed down from generation to generation of sheep, and I am quite prepared to believe it, for we all know that once a hen-bird makes up her mind to build in a certain place nothing on earth will stop her."

Peter thought of Bessy and her polythene and

he began to wonder if she really had gone back to seek for it in the garden of his old home. It was getting quite dark outside now and the lights would be on in the house. Max would be home and the yellow-haired one would be telling him everything that had happened during the day. That had been the time when both of them had come up to his cage and started to talk to him together. *Who's a pretty boy, then? Mary had a little lamb.* "Baa, baa, black sheep!" he said suddenly.

The Teller of Tales gave him a stern look. "I hope you are not trying to throw scorn on my story?" he said.

"Oh no, not at all!" apologised Peter. "I think it's a wonderful story. I wish I could have seen it. I have never seen a linnet's nest." He paused for a moment and then said, "I don't think I have ever seen a linnet, if it comes to that."

The Teller of Tales peered at him and then came closer. "Why," he said suddenly, "I thought when I first came in that your shape was somewhat unusual, and now I see that your colour is quite extraordinary, and your head—what a fine bird you are!"

"Thank you," said Peter modestly.

There was a great flash and the interior of the boathouse was illuminated for a few seconds. Peter's fine feathers seemed to glow like a blue light. All the birds had turned their attention from The Teller of Tales to Peter, but he was unaware of it. The flash had frightened him so much that he had tucked his head under his wing for protection.

"It's only lightning," said Benjy, touching him.

"What's that?" came Peter's muffled voice as a great crash shook the boathouse.

"Thunder," said Julius. "It's all right, Peter, it's only a storm. It will pass over."

"I don't like it."

His voice was drowned as the rain began to beat down from the black sky, and The Teller of Tales had to shout in Peter's ear in order to make himself heard. "What's your name?" he asked.

"Peter."

"Where do you come from?"

"I tort I taw a puddy tat," said Peter miserably.

"He isn't making any sense," said The Teller of Tales to Julius.

"He is to me," said Julius thoughtfully. "I think he's feeling just a little bit homesick!"

"Will you tell me his story?" asked The Teller of Tales. "I'm due to visit my family tomorrow and they'll expect me to have lots to tell them."

Julius began. He was not quite accurate in everything he said, for he had seen Peter's house only from the outside, but Peter kept his head firmly tucked away and didn't interrupt. The storm continued. The air became damp and cold. The water began to rise inside the boathouse. But in spite of everything Peter fell asleep. When he awoke in the early dawn the storm had subsided and The Teller of Tales was gone.

8

The Linnets

"But everything is so damp!" protested Peter. "I do wish the sun would shine!"

"You'll get used to it in time," Julius assured him. "It has to rain occasionally, you know."

The three birds were feeding in the meadow, but Peter wasn't enjoying the food, and every time he moved from one place to another a shower of raindrops fell upon him from the stems of grass. Try as he might to put it out of his mind, he couldn't help thinking of his seed pot, which was never empty—those delicious seeds! If only he could go back just for a visit! If only he had the liberty to come and go as he pleased he wouldn't mind the damp and the cold.

A sudden, dreadful thought occurred to him. "Oh, Julius!" he exclaimed.

"What is it?" asked Julius in concern.

"What if they've got another one?" cried Peter.

"Another what?" asked Julius.

"Who?" put in Benjy.

"My people. Another budgerigar. What if they've got another one and he's sitting in *my* cage at this very moment, eating *my* seeds and ringing *my* little bell?" And Peter hunched himself up into his feathers and stared miserably at a green caterpillar that was edging its way along a leaf.

"Do you really care?" asked Benjy, staring at him in surprise.

"Well, of course I care! It's my cage, isn't it? Just like your tree. You know very well that you don't like other birds sitting in your tree. That's exactly how I feel about my cage."

"But I keep going back to my tree!" said Benjy. "It's part of my territory."

Julius went close to Peter and put out a sympathetic wing. "Do you want to go back, Peter?" he asked gently. "We shall quite understand if you say that you do."

"No," said Peter, "at least, I don't know. Not just yet. I like it so much out here when the sun shines and there are no hawks about and I can talk in bird-language to all the other birds, but then something horrid happens and I feel that I would like to go back until everything is pleasant again."

"Life isn't like that," said Benjy, "not out here."

A strange but sweet voice interrupted the conversation. "Excuse me, but are you Peter the budgerigar?" it asked.

The speaker was a small brown bird with the beak of a seed-eater, somewhat similar to the sparrows, an elegant little bird with a sharp eye. She was perching quite close to them on a flat stone.

"Yes?" said Peter.

"I thought you must be. You were described to me in great detail and, do you know, I didn't believe a word of it. I thought that The Teller of Tales was letting his imagination run away with him as usual."

"The Teller of Tales described me to you?" asked Peter in surprise.

"That's right," went on the linnet, looking at Peter with undisguised admiration. "In fact, he asked me to look for you."

"Why?"

"He told me that you had never seen a linnet."

"Are you a linnet?"

"Yes, I am."

"It's very kind of you to have taken the trouble," said Peter. "And I'm very much obliged to The Teller of Tales for getting in touch with you." He paused, looking shyly at the pretty little bird, then he continued, "The Teller of Tales was telling us about the linnet's nest in a sheep's fleece. Have you heard the story?"

"Many times," the linnet replied. "It is the first story we are told when we are nestlings and the first story we tell to our own young ones."

"Do you believe it?" broke in Benjy.

"I see no reason not to," was the quiet answer. "Birds have nested in stranger places."

"Have you?" asked Julius.

The linnet shook her head. "Oh no," she said, "I'm one of the less adventurous ones. I always nest in the thicket over there."

Peter took a deep breath. "Do you think it would be asking too much of you to let us see it?" he asked. "I should so much like to. I saw a moorhen's nest a few days ago, but I have never seen the nest of a small bird like ourselves. I was brought up in a box."

"A box!" exclaimed the linnet. "Oh, you poor thing—of course you must see my nest. Follow me."

They had to push their way through dense undergrowth in order to reach the nest, and when they finally arrived the three friends were surprised to see a male bird sitting on the eggs. He blinked at his visitors but made no sign of moving. "Jarvis," said his wife, "I have brought Peter the budgerigar to see our eggs. Would you mind moving over just for a moment?"

Jarvis made no response until he had carefully inspected every feature of his visitors, then he said, "One hour a day—that's all the time she allows me, did you know that?"

"I beg your pardon?" stammered Peter, to whom the question had been principally addressed.

"One hour to sit on the eggs. One short hour every afternoon. She never lets me sit on them in the mornings, and now she asks me to move over. It's not fair." He turned to his wife and said again, "It's not fair, Nelly."

Nelly sighed. "It would be only for a moment, Jarvis. Surely you can spare that?"

"Do you like sitting on eggs?" asked Peter, who thought it must be quite uncomfortable.

"Well of course I do," said Jarvis sulkily. "Don't you?"

"I don't know," said Peter. "I've never had any eggs to sit on."

Jarvis gave a curious little cough. "Well," he said, "it's all a question of pride, isn't it? Being the one to actually hatch them—it gives a bird a feeling of achievement."

"He's quite right," said Julius. "I had eggs once, but something dreadful happened to them and I've never felt quite the same since."

"I'm sorry, Julius, I didn't know," said Peter.

"*Please*, Jarvis," broke in Nelly in quite a sharp voice. "You can have extra time tomorrow."

"Promise?" said Jarvis. "Will you let me hatch the first one?"

"If you like," sighed Nelly.

Jarvis moved. Peter looked down at the five eggs. They were whitish-blue, speckled with small rusty spots and squiggles, and they were so beautifully arranged in the bottom of the nest that they formed a perfect pattern against the lining of the nest. Peter's admiration was so great, and the linnets' pride so absorbing, that only the two sparrows kept on the alert for danger, and it was Julius who suddenly alerted the others by saying, "There are humans about. I can't see them, but I know they are there."

"Where?" breathed Jarvis, showing remarkable bravery by going back and sitting on the eggs in order to protect them. Nelly prepared to fly away

and decoy the enemy, whoever it might be, but Julius held her back.

"That strange object over there?" he asked, peering through the bushes. "Has it been there long?"

"Oh yes," replied Nelly. "It was there long before we started to build our nest. It seemed quite harmless. It never moves. Why? What do you think it is?"

"I think it's what the humans call a hide," said Julius.

"A hide?"

"Yes," explained Julius, "Grandfather Sparrow took me to see one once. We perched quite close to it and it spoke."

Peter stared at the hide. "I don't see how it could," he said.

"Neither did I," said Julius, "when I went with Grandfather Sparrow, but we distinctly heard it say, 'Only a couple of house sparrows—nothing to get excited about.' Grandfather Sparrow was *furious*, I can tell you. He jumped up and down on top of its head and said all sorts of rude things to it. He couldn't bear to be called only a house sparrow, for in his own opinion he was really rather special."

"He must have been," said Nelly. "I don't think I would care to jump on its head, however harmless it might be."

"The point is," said Jarvis, "does it move? Does it eat eggs?"

"I don't think so," said Julius.

"That's all right, then," said Jarvis.

"Hush!" said Peter. "I heard it speak."

The birds were silent. They kept quite still and waited.

"I tell you it is," said the hide. "It's a blue budgie, and it can't have been out long because it seems in perfect condition."

The birds looked at one another. A murmuring followed from the hide and then the voice spoke again. "I can try it, anyhow. All budgies seem to respond to it. Who's a pretty boy then? Who's a pretty boy?"

All the birds looked at Peter. Peter hardly knew where to put himself. "Time for beddy-byes," he retorted angrily. "God save the Queen. Mary had a little lamb." And in bird language, "Silly old hide. I've come all this way just to get away from all that and what do I find? A bundle of old rags and sticks telling me that I'm a pretty boy. I might as well be at home listening to it in comfort. At least Max dressed a bit more respectably than *that* does." And he kicked the twig he was standing on, out of sheer embarrassment.

"Never mind the budgie," said the hide, in a different voice. "Somebody's sure to pick it up sooner or later. They're perfectly capable of surviving for a long time out in the wild. We're here to record the song of the linnet, remember?"

The two linnets looked at each other. Nelly began to simper. "Record our song?" she whispered to her husband. "Oh, Jarvis, we're going to be famous!"

"Now listen to me," said Jarvis, sticking out his chest and showing his best side to the hide. "I'm the one who does the singing round here, and don't you forget it. Female linnets should be seen and not heard."

"But, Jarvis . . ." began Nelly.

"No buts. You look after the eggs. I sing." And Jarvis moved over to allow his wife to take her place on the eggs.

Not wishing to intrude upon a domestic quarrel the three friends moved off through the undergrowth. The beautiful voice of the linnet followed them as they went. Peter cast one last, baleful look at the hide. "Pretty boy indeed!" he muttered. "Am I never going to get away from it?"

But Julius had seen a wistful look in Peter's eyes and he knew that there was just the beginning of a wish starting to stir in Peter's breast.

9

Mrs Plenty

"I have an idea," said Benjy one morning, when Peter had been at liberty for more than a week.

"Tell us," urged Peter.

"I hope it isn't anything rash," said Julius cautiously. "You've behaved yourself pretty well since Peter joined us, so I hope you're not going to suggest flying over to the old barn again or anything of that sort."

"Not the old barn," responded Benjy slowly.

"Where then?"

"Well, you remember Bessy?"

"Of course I remember Bessy."

"Do you remember her telling us about Mrs Plenty?"

"Yes," said Julius. "The lady who fed her throughout the winter. What about her?"

"We might go and pay her a visit," said Benjy.

"What on earth for?" asked Julius in astonishment. "We have all we need out here."

"We may have," said Benjy. "You and I. We're used to foraging for food in places like this, but I've noticed that Peter is getting thinner."

Julius looked sharply at Peter. Peter looked down at himself. "Do you feel all right, Peter?" asked Julius.

"Yes," said Peter.

"He may feel all right," said Benjy, "but he doesn't seem to enjoy his food. I'd like him to have a treat. Mrs Plenty is sure to have something tasty for him—and for us, too, of course—and—well, it may even be Peter's birthday, and wouldn't it be nice if it was and he could have something special . . ."

"Benjy," said his brother sternly. "If you want to go to Mrs Plenty's why don't you just say so instead of pretending that you want to help Peter? Peter's birthday indeed! What nonsense!"

"Well, it might be," said Benjy petulantly.

"Yes, it might," said Peter wistfully. He had never had a birthday, at least as far as he could remember. "I feel as if it might be. In fact," he went on, warming to the idea, "I'm practically sure that it *is*. It's my birthday!" he called to a passing whitethroat.

"Many happy returns!" sang the whitethroat.

"Well, now that that's established," broke in Julius, unable to repress a chuckle, "what would you like to do on this special day?"

"I'd like to go and see Mrs Plenty," said Peter.

"I thought you might," said Julius.

"Come on then!" cried Benjy.

"How do you know where Mrs Plenty lives?" asked Peter as he flew beside his two friends.

"We'll find Bessy," said Benjy, "and ask her."

"How will you find Bessy?"

Benjy grinned. "If we fly into her territory," he

said, "we won't have to find her. She will find us. Besides," he went on, "we shall be able to hear her. You know what a gossip she is."

Julius said in a warning note, "Bessy's territory is very close to Peter's old house, you know. Are you sure you want to go back there, Peter, and risk being seen by your people?"

"I don't care," said Peter carelessly. "If I don't want to be caught I won't *be* caught. I can fly as fast as anybody now, you know."

Julius said nothing more on the subject. He could see that the idea of going to Mrs Plenty's house and pretending to have a birthday was so firmly fixed in the budgerigar's mind that nothing would take it out. They came into Bessy's territory in a surprisingly short time. Bessy's husband Dixie came out to meet them. "What do you want?" he demanded.

"We want to see Bessy," said Benjy.

"You can't see her," said Dixie. "She's laying an egg."

"*Really*?" exclaimed Peter.

Benjy looked crestfallen. Even he hadn't the courage to disturb a hen that was laying. "We wanted to ask her something," he said.

"You'll have to come back next week," said Dixie.

"Does it take a week to lay an egg?" asked Peter in amazement.

"Of course not," said Dixie.

"We can't wait a week," said Benjy, "because

it's my friend's birthday and he wanted to ask Bessy how to get to Mrs Plenty's house."

Dixie glared at them. "Is that all?" he said, although quite clearly he couldn't understand the connection between Peter's birthday and Mrs Plenty. "Just follow those starlings over there. They're always barging into Mrs Plenty's garden. Why she tolerates them I'll never know, noisy, troublesome things that they are. They haven't even the sense to know that the food is put out for us blackbirds, not for them." He sighed. "But as we can't go over there ourselves today I suppose you might as well share in the feast."

"What feast?" asked Julius, beginning to think that Benjy's idea was not such a bad one, after all.

"There's a feast every day at Mrs Plenty's house," said the blackbird, obviously feeling annoyed because he couldn't be there himself. "Coming, my love," he called to Bessy, who was clucking unseen in the bushes behind him. "Mrs Plenty doesn't just throw out scraps, you know. She gets special food for us; nuts for the tits, bacon and sweet apples for Bessy and me—although those starlings swear that the bacon is theirs—we've had endless arguments over that—and then for the others, of course, she puts out seeds . . ."

"Seeds!" interrupted Peter. "Real seeds, out of a packet?"

"Yes. Those go on the bird table two or three times a day."

"Let's go," said Peter.

They followed two starlings who were discussing Mrs Plenty's garden, and within a few minutes they were perched upon a tree, looking down at the feast. As well as starlings there were thrushes, robins, chaffinches, sparrows, and even a pair of wrens creeping about in the borders.

"Shall we go down?" said Benjy, looking to his brother for guidance.

"Yes, it seems all right," agreed Julius. "Shall we try the bird-table first?"

They flew down. Peter's bright colour seemed to scare away a group of little tree sparrows who had had the bird table all to themselves, and he and his two friends settled down to eat what was laid out before them. "My favourites!" cried Peter, gobbling too fast.

"Don't look now," whispered Julius suddenly, "but there's a human staring at us through the window."

"Staring at Peter," said Benjy, who had already seen the face. "It must be Mrs Plenty, so we needn't be afraid."

They kept on eating for a few minutes, and then Julius, who had kept his eye on the window all the time, said, "She's opening the window."

Peter glanced up. "She looks very pleasant, and very kind," he said, "but I do hope she won't call out 'Who's a pretty boy, then?', not with all those tree sparrows listening."

Mrs Plenty, however, said nothing at all. She simply opened the window as wide as it would go and then disappeared. Peter noticed that it was starting to rain again. Most of the birds had stopped chattering, and quite a number of them were making their way home.

"Are you enjoying your birthday, Peter?" chuckled Benjy. "Shall I ask the song thrush to sing 'Happy Birthday' to you?"

But Peter didn't answer. His whole body had stiffened and he was staring towards the open window as if he had seen a real ghost-bird.

"What is it, Peter?" asked Julius in alarm, spreading his wings a little in case it was necessary to fly away.

"Hush!" was the breathless response. "Can't you hear it?"

Julius and Benjy turned their attention towards the house. Julius said, "Why, it sounds like a . . ." He stopped, hardly daring to say the word.

"It sounds like another budgerigar," said Benjy.

"I haven't seen another budgerigar since I was just a fledgling," Peter whispered. "Oh, I *must* go and look!"

"Be careful, Peter," urged Julius, but the warning wasn't even heard. Peter had already flown towards the window, and as the two sparrows watched he came down on the sill and looked into the room. "Can you see anything?" called Julius.

"Yes, I can see a cage, and there's a green budgerigar in it—a *green* one, Julius."

"Has it got green legs?" cried Benjy delightedly.

"Cheeky old thing!" said the green budgerigar

in human language.

"I beg your pardon," said Peter to the green budgerigar. "I didn't mean to be rude."

"Cheeky old thing!" said the green budgerigar again. "Merry Christmas!" He didn't look in the least offended, so Peter hopped on to the window frame and tried to draw the stranger into bird conversation.

"I do hope I'm not intruding," he said, "but I heard you talking and I simply had to come and have a look at you. Are you happy in there?"

"Yes, of course I am. Are you happy out there?"

"Most of the time," said Peter, "but I don't like it very much when the sparrow-hawk is about or when there's a thunderstorm."

"I know," nodded the green budgerigar. "I tried it myself, once. I was only out a couple of days, but you wouldn't believe the near-misses I had. First of all there was an *enormous*, furry animal, the like of which I have never seen, and then there was . . ."

Benjy and Julius, watching from the bird table, saw Peter hop inside the room. A shadow fell upon the window. A hand reached out and the window snapped shut. The two brothers stared at each other with gaping beaks. "He's been caught," gasped Julius after a moment or two of stunned silence.

"Poor Peter!" sighed Benjy.

Julius looked towards the house. "Oh, I don't know," he murmured slowly. "I think he had been out long enough. I think, deep down, he wanted to go back inside."

"What shall we do now?" asked Benjy, feeling lost and lonely now that Peter had gone.

"There's nothing much that we can do," Julius told him, "except, perhaps, to say goodbye."

They flew bravely over to the window and looked in. Mrs Plenty had Peter on her finger and was just putting him in the cage with the other bird.

"Peter!"

"Yes, Julius?"

"I'm sorry you've been caught."

"Don't worry. At least I have a companion."

"Yes, I'm glad about that."

"Julius."

"Yes, Peter?"

"And Benjy."

"Yes, Peter?"

"Thank you for everything."

"It was a pleasure. We'll come and visit you, often."

"I'd like that. Give my love to all the other birds. I shall have so much to think about during the long, winter evenings."

"Merry Christmas!" said the green budgerigar.

"Merry Christmas!" said Peter.

10

Come Back Peter

Julius and Benjy had decided to go and see Bessy. They found her sitting happily on three eggs. After enquiring politely after her health they told her what had happened to Peter.

"Captured!" she cried, jerking herself upright, so that the two sparrows caught a glimpse of one of her green-blue eggs. "By whom?"

"Er—by Mrs Plenty, actually," said Benjy.

She nodded sharply. "I heard you were enquiring for Mrs Plenty," she said. "Well, that's all right. Mrs Plenty will be good to him. There's only one thing that worries me."

"And what is that?" asked Julius.

"You remember how I came to you that day and asked Peter if he knew where I could get some polythene?"

"Yes," said Julius, "and I see that you did get some."

"And very smart it looks, too," chirped Benjy, looking at the nest.

Bessy continued, "I found it where Peter said I might, and I was just about to fly back here with it when those two came out into the garden."

"You mean Peter's old humans?" Julius said.

"Those two. They had come out to look for him.

They had his cage with them, and packets of seeds, and they rang his little bell and called his name. They were very upset. I have never been so sorry for anybody in my life." She settled herself back on to her eggs. "I thought I ought to tell you, because it proves that even though Peter felt he had to get away from them, they were very fond of him."

"Yes. Thank you," said Julius thoughtfully.

"Now, if you will excuse me, I think I shall lay another egg. I find three a most uncomfortable number."

The two sparrows flew hurriedly away. "Do you think we ought to tell him?" asked Benjy.

"Oh we must," said Julius. "He ought to know."

When they arrived at Mrs Plenty's house Peter was telling his companion about The Teller of Tales, but when he heard Julius and Benjy calling to him he responded immediately. Julius told him what Bessy had seen. He was hardly prepared for Peter's reaction.

"Oh, Julius!" said the budgerigar in great distress. "I never once thought of that! All the time I was out I didn't give them a thought. It never occurred to me that they might be unhappy because I had flown away. How could I be so unkind?" And he withdrew to a corner of the cage, wrapped in misery.

The two sparrows did their best to comfort him, and the green budgerigar even offered to let Peter climb his little ladder, which so far he had not been allowed to do, but nothing seemed to make Peter feel any better. He simply sat there muttering to himself and staring into space.

The sparrows had just decided between themselves to go and ask the linnet to come and cheer him up when Peter suddenly began to hop about the cage. He seemed very excited and he was repeating all his old phrases, one after another, so that the green budgerigar had almost begun to think that he was showing off.

"What *is* all the noise about?" cried Mrs Plenty, coming into the room and presenting a smiling face to Peter. "What is your name, I wonder?"

"Mary had a little lamb," said Peter. "Time for beddy-byes. Seven-eight-three-o-six-five one."

Mrs Plenty gave a startled exclamation. "*What* was that?" she said.

"I tort I taw a puddy tat. Seven-eight-three-o-six-five-one."

Mrs Plenty left the room in a great hurry.

"You seem to have offended her," said Peter's companion.

Peter began to whistle. Mrs Plenty's voice could just be heard, apparently talking to herself. "And I thought it couldn't possibly be," she was saying, "but he said it so clearly. Peter, you say? Yes, definitely a sky-blue. And he said he thought he saw a pussy cat. It is? I'll bring him round."

After a few more minutes Mrs Plenty came back into the room carrying an empty cage. "So you are Peter," she said. "You're a very clever little chap, do you know that?"

"Clever boy, clever boy," said Peter.

Mrs Plenty put her hand into the cage and took Peter out. "You're going home, Peter," she said, placing him in the empty cage. "They'll be so pleased to see you."

Benjy began to hop up and down on the window ledge. He was almost as excited as Peter himself. A few minutes later Mrs Plenty came out of the house carrying Peter in his cage. The sparrows flew up on to the guttering to watch what she was doing. She went into a small building attached to the house. "Why has she taken him in there?" said Benjy in alarm. "That's not where he lives."

There were strange noises and then Julius said, "I know what it is. It's one of those motor cars. She's going to take Peter home in that."

"Let's follow her!" said Benjy. His eyes were alight with excitement.

"I'm not sure that we ought to," said Julius. "She might think it rather rude."

"Never mind what she thinks!" cried Benjy recklessly. "It's Peter who matters. I'm sure he'd like us to be there when he comes home."

"You're right," agreed Julius. "We've been with him throughout all his adventures; it's only right that we should see them through to the end. Come on—there she goes!"

The car backed down the drive and out into the road. Julius caught a brief glimpse of his friend sitting on a perch in the middle of the cage, which had been placed on the back seat of the car. He was hanging on to something with his beak, and his toes were firmly wrapped round the wooden perch. "I don't think I should care to travel in that," said Benjy as they flew overhead, high above the street lamps.

"Watch out for that high building!" said Julius. "You guide me; I'm watching the car."

Not a soul gave them a second glance as they twisted and turned after the car, and even when it came to a stop outside Peter's house the two sparrows were not even casually noticed. "They've had their house painted," Julius observed. "It was brown when Peter flew away, and now it's bright green. They must have done that to cheer themselves up."

They flew to the top of the old dead tree and waited until they could see movements inside the room where Peter's old cage had been, then they took a perch on a drainpipe near the window. "We ought to give him time to get used to being back before we speak to him," whispered Julius.

"And we must make sure that the humans have left the room, too," agreed Benjy.

The window was open and Mrs Plenty's voice could be heard saying goodbye. "Do make sure that the window is closed before you let him out again," she laughed. "That's a very adventurous budgie you've got there."

There was silence. The two sparrows hopped nearer. Still they could hear nothing. Benjy ventured to place his foot on the window frame. "I do wish you wouldn't be so rash!" cried Julius in alarm.

"Julius, is that you?" came Peter's voice.

"Yes," said Julius. "Are you all right, Peter?"

"Yes, thank you." There was a pause. "Julius," he went on.

"Yes, Peter?"

"I've got a new cage."

"That's nice."

"Is it a better one, Peter?" asked Benjy, peering into the room. "I can't see it."

"It's over here."

Benjy was almost in the room before he saw the cage, and then he said, "Oh yes, I see it. Oh! OH!!!"

"What is it, Benjy? What's the matter?" asked his brother in alarm.

"They *did* get another budgerigar," said Benjy.

"Oh, Peter, I'm so sorry," said Julius, "but I'm sure they love you just the same."

There was an awkward silence, and then a sweet budgerigar voice said, "Peter, may I look in your mirror?"

The two sparrows stared at each other. "It's a *lady* budgerigar!" they gasped.

Some time later the sparrows were back on the old dead tree. They had said goodbye to Peter after receiving his grateful thanks for a wonderful adventure, and had left him telling his new companion all about it. "He won't be lonely now,

will he?" said Benjy, looking back at the house.

"No, but we must stick to our promise to visit him regularly," said Julius.

"Of course."

Julius suddenly looked amused. "Benjy," he said, "I have something to tell you."

"What is it?"

"You've got green legs."

"I have? I *have*! How did that happen?"

"Wet paint on the window frame. That's why it was left wide open."

The two brothers rocked with laughter. "I'll tell you what," spluttered Benjy after a while, "let's go and show the moorhen."

"Yes," agreed Julius at once, "let's do that."

And they flew away over the river.